Do you know what the fastest skiing speed is? Learn more on page 26.

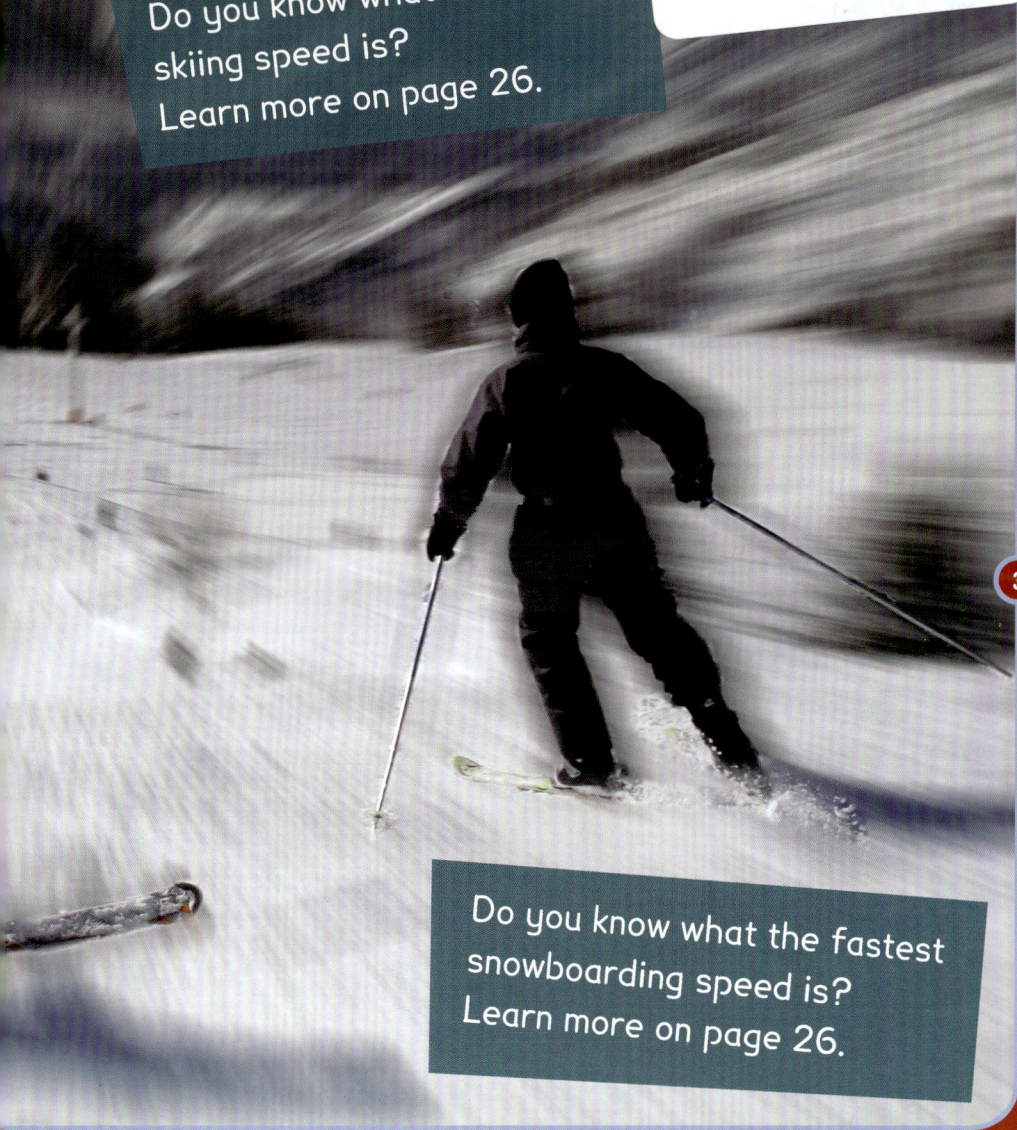

Do you know what the fastest snowboarding speed is? Learn more on page 26.

3

position	skiing	slope	speed
puh-ZISH-uhn	SKEE-ing	SLOHP	SPEED

Need For Speed

WRITTEN BY JULIE ELLIS

Do you like to go really fast?
How about zooming down a mountain
with a long board strapped to each foot, or **skiing**?

Imagine you are in the snow.
The tip of your nose is really cold.
You must wear gloves and a woollen hat.
The snow crunches under your skis.

4

WINTER SPORTS

Do you know what position is?
Check out page 5.

Do you know what motion is?
Turn to page 6.

Do you know what distance is?
Find out on page 7.

Read these words then check out pages 30 and 31.

distance	luge	moguls	motion
DIS-tuhns	LOOJ	MOH-guhlz	MOH-shuhn

Where are you?
You are on the side
of a mountain, or a **slope**.
Below you, there are hills.
Behind, there are mountains.
Where you are in a place
is your **position**.

Position

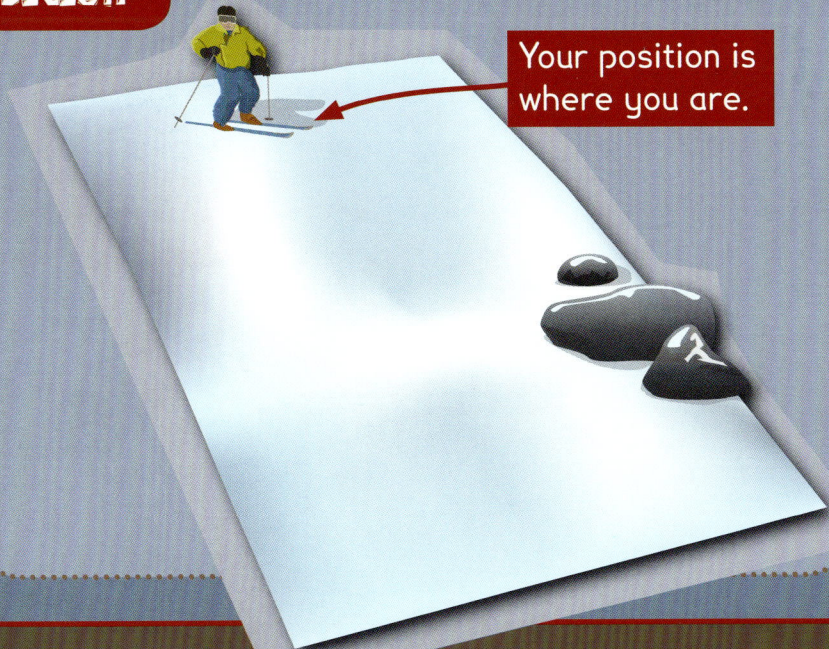

Your position is
where you are.

Use your poles to push off.
Now you are moving slowly.
You were standing on the slope.
Now you are skiing down the slope.
When your position changes, you are in **motion**.

Motion

If you are moving,
you are in motion.

Whoa! Watch where you're going!
Look out for that man in front of you!

You are still skiing down the slope.
You are moving faster now.
You are moving past rocks.
You are moving past ski lifts.
In time, you will come to the bottom of the slope.
The measure of how far it is from one place
to another place is known as **distance**.

Distance

Distance is how far it is from one place to another.

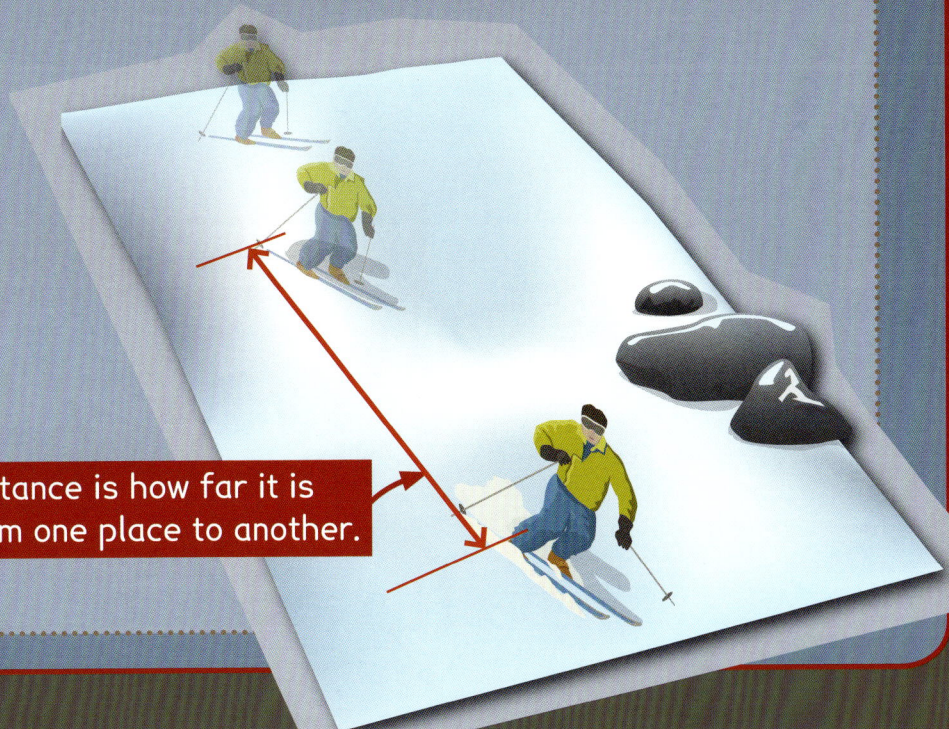

How fast are you moving?
You are moving faster now.
You are tearing down the slope.
The distance you travel
in a certain amount of time is your **speed**.
Your speed tells how slow or fast
you are moving down the slope.
The speed you reach as you cut
through the cold air hurts your nose.

Speed

Your speed is the distance you travel in a certain time.

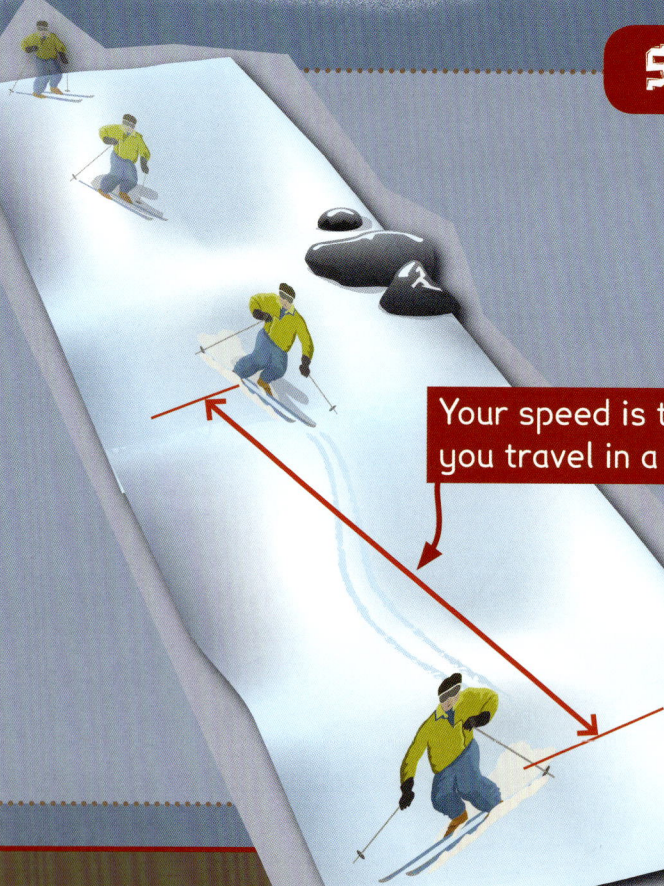

You are near the bottom of the slope.
Now it is time to slow down.
Instead of skiing a straight line,
you must zigzag down the slope.
Use your skis to turn to the right.
Use your skis to turn to the left.

Congratulations!
You made it to the bottom of the slope.
What an awesome run!
You owned that mountain.
Carve up those slopes!

Read on to find out more about speed. →

Race against TIME

written by Julie Ellis

START

Question:

Two girls are having a race.
One girl skis straight down the slope.
The other girl zigzags down the slope.
Which girl wins the race?

Answer:
The girl who skis straight down the slope wins the race.

She travels a shorter distance.
She travels at a faster speed.

The girl who zigzags down the slope travels a longer distance.
She travels at a slower speed.
She does not win the race.

START

11

Finish

Finish

Read on to find out about some cool winter sports. →

Moving in All Directions

Written by Julie Ellis

Ice Climbers

Ice climbers climb mountains.
Ice climbers use tools to climb.
They use ice axes in their hands
and crampons on their boots.
Ice climbers move very slowly.
They must find the safest way
to the top of the mountain.

An ice climber moves
slowly up a mountain.

Speed Skiers

Speed skiers ski in a straight line.
The course they ski has no turns.
They move very fast down a slope.
The skier with the fastest time wins.

A disabled skier moves quickly down a slope.

Figure-Skaters

Figure-skaters skate in a circle.
They move around and around.
They spin in circles very quickly.

Figure-skaters spin
around and around.

Slalom Skiers

Slalom skiers ski down a slope.
They move between poles.
They change direction many times.
They move very fast down the slope.
The skier with the fastest time wins.

A slalom skier zigzags down a slope.

Luge Riders

A sled that a person lies on is a **luge**.
The person rides the luge feet first.
A luge track has straight runs.
It has many curves and bends, too.
Luge riders change direction each time
they round the bends in the track.
The luge rider with the fastest time wins.

A luge rider travels on a track
with straight runs and bends.

Ice Hockey Players

Ice hockey players move in all directions.
They chase after a small rubber disc.
The small rubber disc is called a puck.
There are two teams of players.
They hit the puck with their sticks.
They try to hit the puck into a goal.
The team with the most goals wins.

Ice hockey players move in all directions.

Read on to see what happens when a surfer takes his board to the snow. →

The Snow Surfer

Written by John Suzuki • Illustrated by Dougal Borman

Surfer Dude is a competitive surfer. Today, he has won the championships.

Wow, Surfer Dude! You're the champion!

I know, Marina. I know.

18

I've mastered surfing. I own the waves! I need a new challenge.

Like what?

Think about it. What's something totally different from surfing?

Uhh...watching TV?
No, I'm going to master the snow.
But you don't know how to ski.
Surfing, skiing. They're both about motion.
If you understand motion, you can control your board. It doesn't matter if it's on water or snow.
You're going to use your surfboard on the snow?
Sure, why not? What are bumps in the snow?

But if I plan my position right, I'll catch the wave.

Yes, but...

The next thing is distance. Distance is how far it is from one place to another.

21

If I know the distance, I can plan how to get there.

Sure, sure. But listen...

The last thing is speed. Speed is the distance I'll cover in a certain time.

And now, champion surfer Surfer Dude will show us his amazing snow surfing!

See, it's all about motion. Water moves. Snow doesn't. That's why the position of Surfer Dude and the position of his board are different now. The distance is how far he got before he wiped out off his board. The speed is how fast he moved through the air before he hit the snow face first.

See what I mean? I think you'd better stick to riding waves after all, Surfer Dude.

23

Read on to find out more about winter sports. →

Multimedia Information

FAQS

Q What are *regular* and *goofy*?

A All snowboarders are *regular* or *goofy*.
Do you stand with your left foot on the front
of the board? Then you're *regular*.
Do you stand with your right foot on the front
of the board? Then you're *goofy*.

Regular

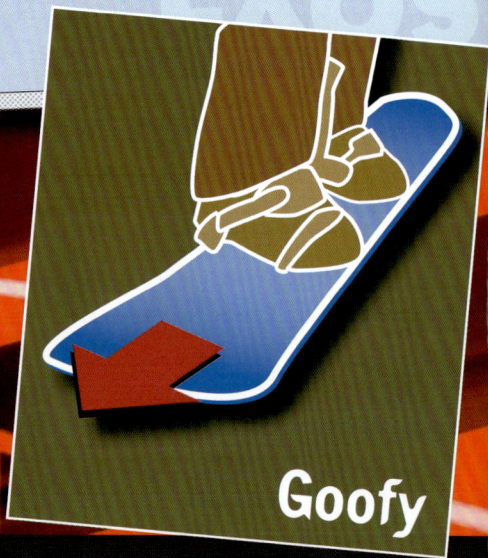

Goofy

Snowy Mountain Ski Resort

SERIOUS ACTION   SERIOUS THRILLS

Trails for learners and pros

Ski and board school on-site

Snowy Mountain Ski Resort

Learn all the best tricks and techniques.

HOW FAST IS FAST?

Speed Skating – Joji Kato
(Japan) (500 m) World Champs,
2005, USA – 52.5 kph

Luging – Armin Zoggeler
(Italy) Torino Olympics,
2006, Italy – 135.5 kph

Airboarding – Laurent Matthey
(Switzerland) Open Gils,
2005, France – 141.7 kph

Snowboarding – Darren Powell
(Australia) World Champs,
1999, France – 201.9 kph

Snow Cycling – Eric Barone
(France) Les Arcs,
2000, France – 222.2 kph

Speed Skiing – Philippe Goitschel
(France) Les Arcs,
2002, France – 250.7 kph

0   50   100   150   200   250
kilometres per hour

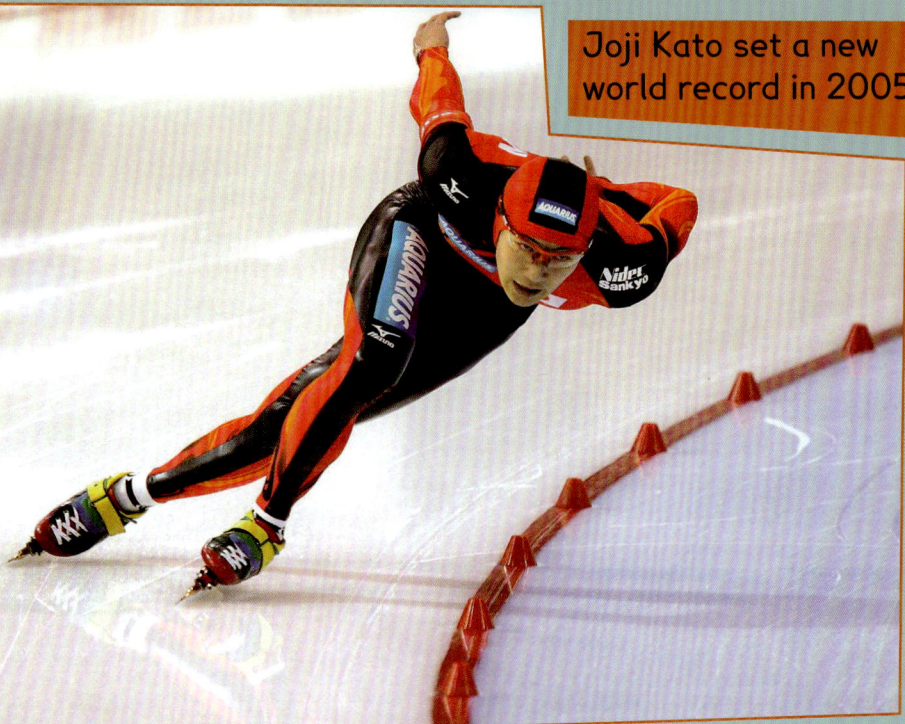

Joji Kato set a new world record in 2005.

Eric Barone cycles down the track of Les Arcs.

Turn the page to check what you have learned. ➡

8

Quick

Quiz

1. What is the word for where you are?

2. What are you doing when your position changes?

3. What tells how far it is from one place to another place?

4. What tells how fast or slow you are moving?

5. What ways do speed skiers move?

6. What ways do luge riders move?

7. What is the fastest snowboarding speed?

8. What is the fastest skiing speed?

Turn to page 32 for clues. →

Learn More

Choose Your Topic
Choose one winter sport in this book.

Research Your Topic
Find out more about your sport.
Find out all the interesting things you can about the sport.
Find out all the interesting things you can about the people who do the sport.

Write Your Article
You may need to make notes first.
You may need to draw maps.
You may need to find photos.
You may need to draw diagrams.
Get your facts in order.
Use subheadings to help you do this.
Write a draft.
Check your spelling.
Check your punctuation.

Present Your Topic
Share your work with other members of your group.

distance – how far it is from one place to another place

luge – a sled that a person rides feet first

moguls – bumps in the snow

motion – movement

position – where something or someone is in a place

skiing – a winter sport where people travel over snow on skis strapped to their feet

slope – a part of the side of a mountain that a skier travels down

speed – distance travelled in a certain time

Index

Clues to the
Quick 8 Quiz

1. Go to page 5.
2. Go to page 6.
3. Go to page 7.
4. Go to page 8.
5. Go to page 13.
6. Go to page 16.
7. Go to page 26.
8. Go to page 26.